# English-Korean Picture Dictionary

Frances M. Koh

illustrated by Denise S. Vignes

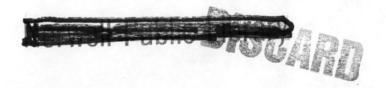

**East West Press**

P.O. Box 14149, Minneapolis, Minnesota 55414

First Edition 1988
Second Printing 1989
Revised Edition 1992

Text and cover illustrations by Denise S. Vignes
Text and cover design by Frances M. Koh

ISBN 0-9606090-3-2
Library of Congress Catalog Card Number 87-83309

Printed in the United States of America.
10 9 8 7 6 5 4 3 2 1

# CONTENTS

# PREFACE

After the publication of <u>Oriental Children in American Homes</u>, a number of adoptive parents of Korean-born children wrote urging me to publish a dictionary that would help their children learn both Korean and English words through the use of pictures.

Thus came the publication of this dictionary. It is designed to aid Korean-speaking children to learn some basic English words, and their adoptive parents to learn basic everyday phrases that can be helpful in communicating with their children.

Moreover, parents or a classroom teacher or tutor will also find the dictionary useful in teaching the students English or Korean as a second language.

Frances M. Koh

# INTRODUCTION

## The Korean Letters and Their Sounds

Throughout this book, things are identified first in English, then by the romanized Korean equivalents, which are followed by Korean orthography (han-gŭl). There are five known romanization systems by which Korean letters and sounds are romanized, that is spelled in English alphabet.  In this book, Korean letters and sounds are romanized according to a modified version of McCune-Reischauer system.*

### A.  Vowels

#### 1.  Simple Vowels

| Korean letter | M-R Romanization (modified) | English sound (approximate) |
| --- | --- | --- |
| ㅏ | a | as the a of "father" |
| ㅑ | ya | as the ya of "yard" |
| ㅓ | ŏ | as the u of "but" |
| ㅕ | yŏ | as the yea of "yearn" |
| ㅗ | o | as the o of "horn" |
| ㅛ | yo | as the yo of "yoga" |
| ㅜ | u | as the ou of "you" |
| ㅠ | yu | as the u of "use" |
| ㅡ | ŭ | as the u of "urn" |
| ㅣ | i | as the i of "hit" and sometimes as the i of "meet" |

#### 2.  Diphthongs

| Korean letter | M-R Romanization (modified) | English sound (approximate) |
| --- | --- | --- |
| ㅐ | ae | as the a of "cat" |
| ㅒ | yae | as the ya of "yam" |
| ㅔ | e | as the e of "get" |
| ㅖ | ye | as the ye of "yet" |
| ㅚ | oe | as the we of "wet" |
| ㅟ | wi | as the wie of "wield" |
| ㅢ | ŭi | as the u of "fur" plus e of "even" |
| ㅘ | wa | as the wa of "wad" |
| ㅝ | wŏ | as the wo of "wonder" |
| ㅙ | wae | as the wa of "wagon" |
| ㅞ | we | as the we of "web" |

---

* Also refer to Standard English-Korean Dictionary by B.J. Jones or English-Korean Dictionary by Joan V. Underwood.

B.   Consonants

1.   Simple Consonants

| Korean letter | M-R Romanization (modified) | | | English sound (approximate) |
|---|---|---|---|---|
| | initial | medial | final | |
| ㄱ | k | g | k | as the k of "kin" or the g of "go" |
| ㄴ | n | n | n | as the n of "net" |
| ㄷ | t | d | t | as the t of "to" or the d of "do" |
| ㄹ | r | r | l | as the l of "leg" or the r of "red" |
| ㅁ | m | m | m | as the m of "money" |
| ㅂ | p | b | p | as the p of "pot" or the b of "bed" |
| ㅅ | s | s | t | as the s of "sit" |
| ㅇ | -ng | | | as the -ng of "sing" |
| ㅈ | ch | j | t | as the j of "joy" |
| ㅊ | ch' | ch' | t | more aspirate than the ch of "choice" |
| ㅋ | k' | k' | k | more aspirate than the k of "king" |
| ㅌ | t' | t' | t | more aspirate than the t of "turkey" |
| ㅍ | p' | p' | p | more aspirate than the p of "pull" |
| ㅎ | h | h | - | as the h of "hair" |

In the simple consonants listed above, a Korean sound is assigned to English sounds in terms of its position in a Korean word.  For example, if Korean sound "ㄷ" occurs in the initial syllable of a Korean word, English letter "t" is assigned.  If the same sound occurs in the medial syllable, English letter "d" is assigned.

| Example: | Korean word | M-R Rom (modifed) | English word |
|---|---|---|---|
| | 단 단 한 | tan-dan-han | tight |

2.   Double Consonants

| Korean letter | M-R Romanization (modified) | | | English sound (approximate) |
|---|---|---|---|---|
| | initial | medial | final | |
| ㄲ | kk | gg | k | stronger sound than one "g" and produced with a force in the throat. |
| ㄸ | tt | dd | - | stronger sound than one "d" and produced by pressing the tongue against the front teeth and exerting a force in the throat. |
| ㅃ | pp | bb | - | stronger sound than one "b" and produced with tightened lip muscles. |
| ㅆ | ss | ss | t | stronger sound than one "s" and produced by pressing the tongue against the lower front teeth. |
| ㅉ | jj | jj | - | stronger sound than one "j" and produced with tightened tongue pressing against the upper front teeth and tightened mouth muscles. |

Beside the double consonants listed above, there are mixed double consonants, such as ㄼ, ㄿ, ㄻ, ㅀ, ㅄ, ㄵ , etc.  The sound changes of these mixed double consonants are rather complicated, but there are relatively few of them.  For example, the Korean word for "wide" consists of two Korean syllables and the first syllable has mixed double consonants.

Example:  <u>Korean word</u>  <u>M-R Rom. (modified)</u>  <u>English</u>

넓은  nŏl-bŭn  wide

In the above case, the first consonant (ㄹ) is pronounced as part of the first syllable of the word and the second consonant (ㅂ) is pronounced as part of the second syllable of the word.  The second syllable of a word with mixed double consonants often starts with Korean vowel "o" (-ng).

The Korean language contains a number of sounds which do not occur in English, and vice versa.  For example, the sound (ㄹ) of the Korean alphabet has no English equivalent, but it falls somewhere near the English sounds of "r" and "l."  (For this reason, in the McCune-Reischauer system, the Korean sound 【ㄹ】 is assigned to English sound "r" and "l," either of which is to be used according to the sound position in a Korean word.)  Because the Korean language doesn't have the exact sound of English "r" or "l," Koreans tend to have difficulty in pronouncing English sound "r" or "l" accurately, as well as they tend to confuse the two sounds when pronouncing them.

Romanization systems such as McCune-Reischauer system were invented presumably to aid those English-speaking persons who wish to learn to speak Korean words or phrases in a hurry or on an elementary level.  Since the Korean phonetic system is far more complicated than others, such as that of Japanese, anyone who is seriously interested in mastering the Korean language is advised to learn the language from Korean orthography (han-gŭl) rather than from a romanized Korean.

Although some editors do not hypenate romanized Korean words, romanized Korean words in this book are hypenated between individual syllables for easy pronunciation and clarity.

Grammar

Korean grammar is drastically different from that of English.  Although discussion of the grammar is beyond the scope of these pages, a few words can be said about the basic differences in sentence structure between English and Korean.  In the Korean sentence, as in the English, the subject comes at the beginning of a sentence.  However, the word order in the predicate is completely the reverse of the English sentence, with an object preceding a verb.

Example:  I am going to school.

Na-nŭn hak-kyo e kan-da.
(I)  (school)  (am going)

In the above Korean sentence there is no preposition before the noun "hak-kyo," but it is followed by a post-positional particle "e."  In a way the post-positional particle "e" serves the same function as the English preposition "to" in indicating a noun's case.

Anyone who wishes to learn more about the Korean language may refer to the language section of <u>Oriental Children in American Homes: How Do They Adjust?</u> by Frances M. Koh (East West Press, 1981).

| | | | |
|---|---|---|---|
| 1. | runway | hwal-ju-ro | 활주로 |
| 2. | airplane | pi-haeng-gi | 비행기 |
| 3. | wing | nal-gae | 날개 |
| 4. | jet engine | che-t'ŭ ki-gwan | 제트기관 |
| 5. | tail/tail fin | kko-ri | 꼬리 |
| 6. | luggage/baggage maintenance person | su-ha-mul ch'ŏ-ri-in | 수하물처리인 |
| 7. | truck | t'ŭ-rŏk | 트럭 |
| 8. | (flight) schedule board | (pi-haeng) si-gan-pan | (비행)시간판 |
| 9. | ticket agent | p'yo p'a-nŭn-sa-ram | 표파는사람 |
| 10. | ticket counter | p'yo p'a-nŭn-dae | 표파는대 |
| 11. | passenger | yŏ-gaek | 여객 |
| 12. | girl | so-nyŏ | 소녀 |
| 13. | luggage | ka-bang | 가방 |

| | | |
|---|---|---|
| 1. | grandfather | ha-ra-bŏ-ji | 할아버지 |
| 2. | grandmother | hal-mŏ-ni | 할머니 |
| 3. | father | a-bba/a-bŏ-ji | 아빠/아버지 |
| 4. | mother | ŏm-ma/ŏ-mŏ-ni | 엄마/어머니 |
| 5. | (younger) sister | yŏ-dong-seng | 여동생 |
| 6. | (younger) brother | nam-dong-seng | 남동생 |
| 7. | (older) sister | (for women) ŏn-ni | 언니 |
| | | (for men) nu-nim | 누님 |
| 8. | (older) brother | (for women) o-bba | 오빠 |
| | | (for men) hyŏng-nim | 형님 |
| 9. | aunt (father's sister) | ko-mo | 고모 |
| | (mother's sister) | i-mo | 이모 |
| | (uncle's wife) | suk-mo, a-ju-mŏ-ni | 숙모,아주머니 |

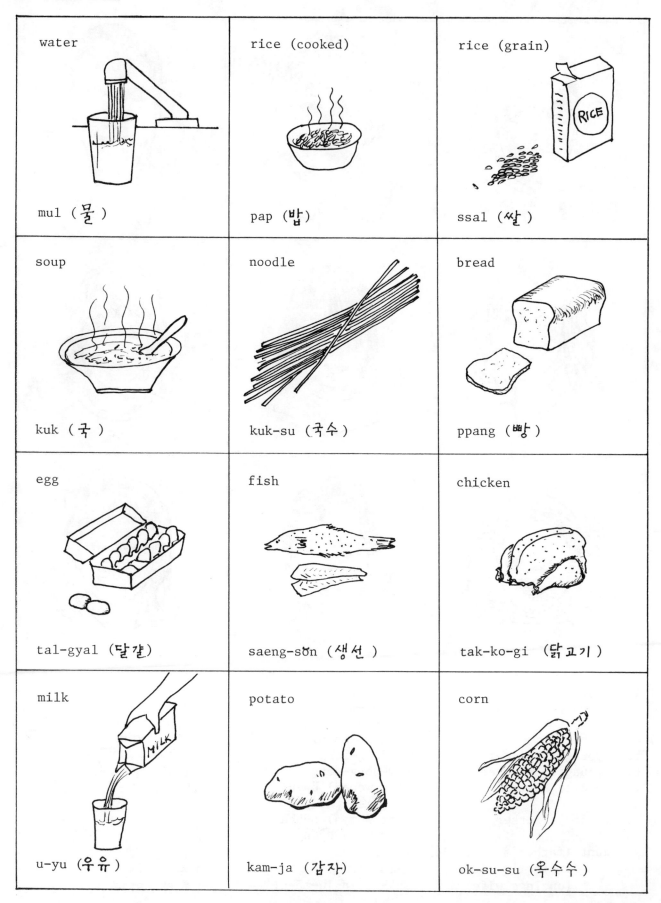

| | | |
|---|---|---|
| water | rice (cooked) | rice (grain) |
| mul （물） | pap （밥） | ssal （쌀） |
| soup | noodle | bread |
| kuk （국） | kuk-su （국수） | ppang （빵） |
| egg | fish | chicken |
| tal-gyal （달걀） | saeng-sŏn （생선） | tak-ko-gi （닭고기） |
| milk | potato | corn |
| u-yu （우유） | kam-ja （감자） | ok-su-su （옥수수） |

cucumber

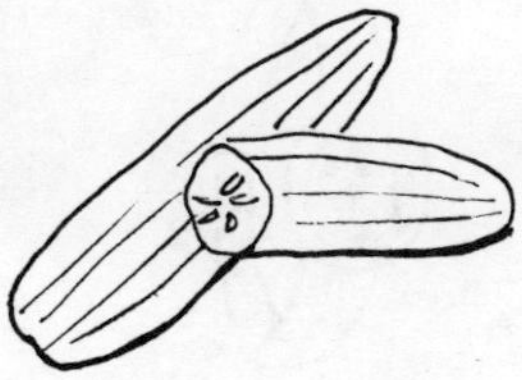

o-i (오이)

onion

yang-p'a (양파)

sweet potato

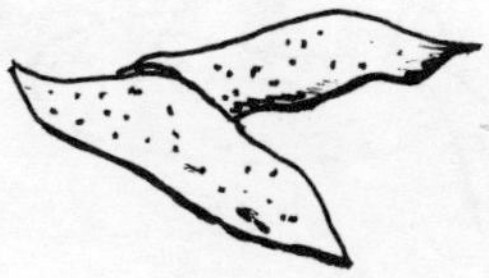

ko-gu-ma (고구마)

peas

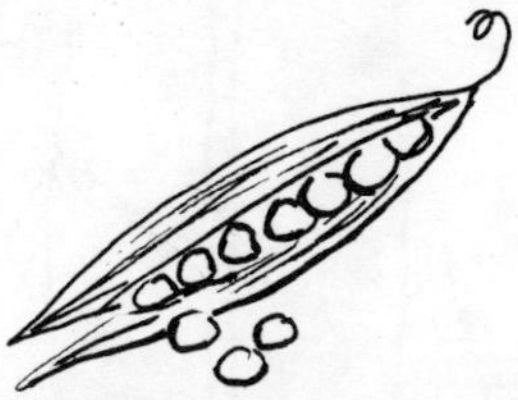

wan-du-k'ong (완두콩)

carrot

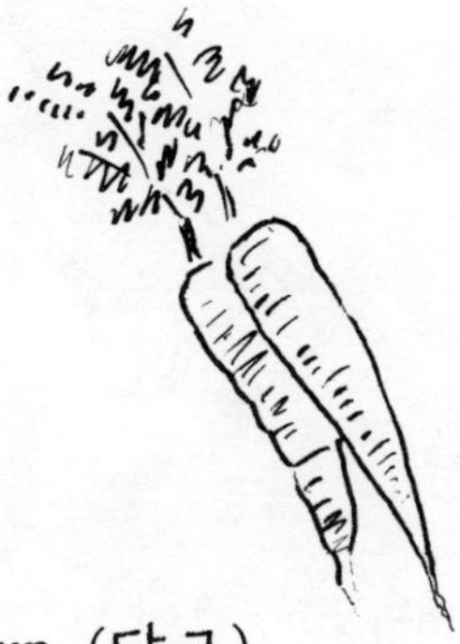

tang-gun (당근)

tomato

t'o-ma-t'o (토마토)

watermelon

su-bak (수박)

peach

pok-sung-a (복숭아)

strawberry

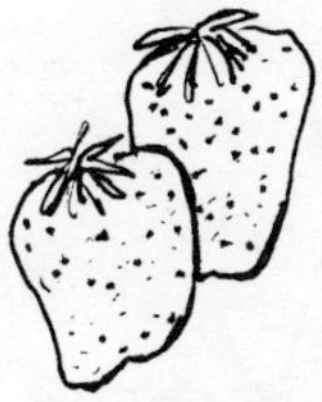

ddal-gi (딸기)

banana

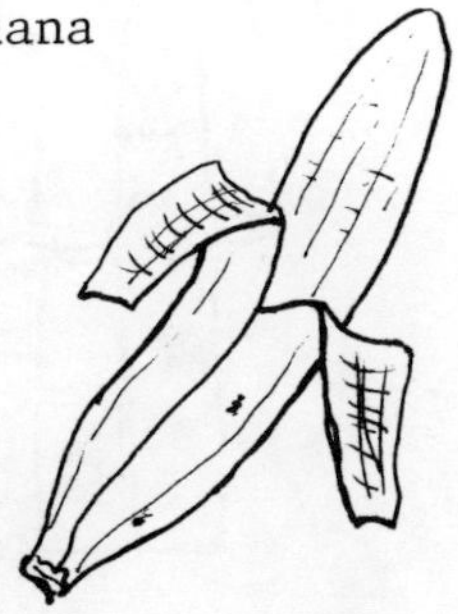

pa-na-na (바나나)

apple

sa-gwa (사과)

grape

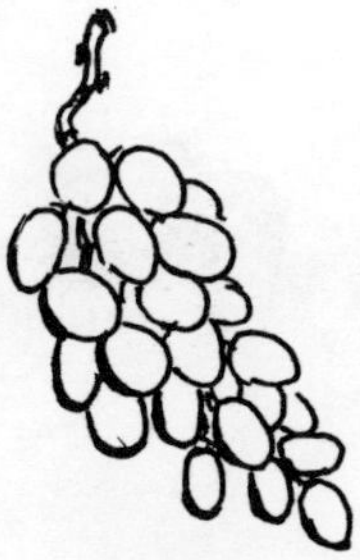

p'o-do (포도)

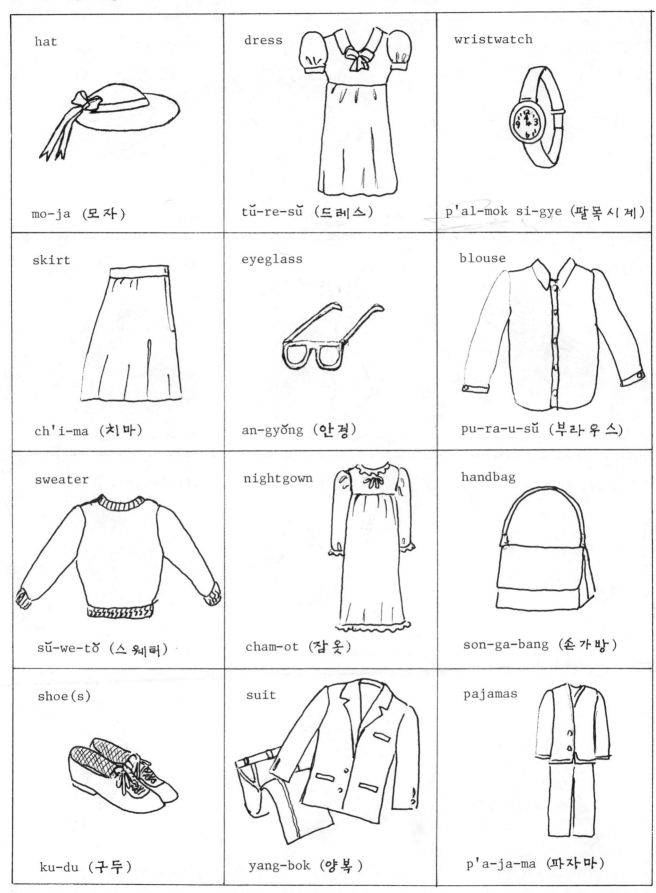

| | | |
|---|---|---|
| hat<br>mo-ja (모자) | dress<br>tŭ-re-sŭ (드레스) | wristwatch<br>p'al-mok si-gye (팔목시계) |
| skirt<br>ch'i-ma (치마) | eyeglass<br>an-gyŏng (안경) | blouse<br>pu-ra-u-sŭ (부라우스) |
| sweater<br>sŭ-we-tŏ (스웨터) | nightgown<br>cham-ot (잠옷) | handbag<br>son-ga-bang (손가방) |
| shoe(s)<br>ku-du (구두) | suit<br>yang-bok (양복) | pajamas<br>p'a-ja-ma (파자마) |

sport hat

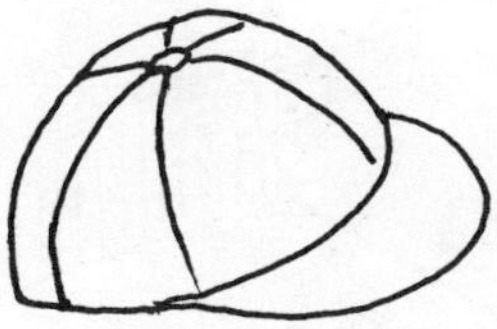

un-dong mo-ja (운동모자)

jacket

cha-k'et (자켓)

sneaker(s)

un-dong-hwa (운동화)

sock(s)

yang-mal (양말)

glove(s)

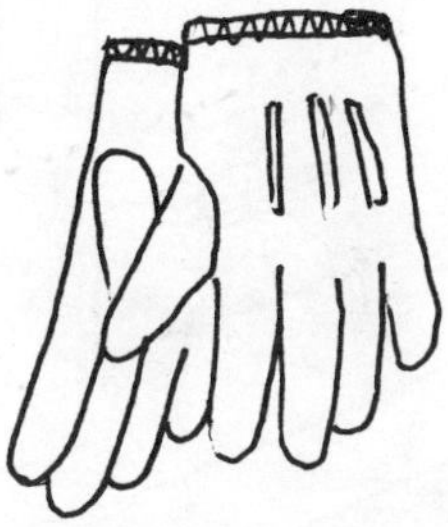

chang-gap (장갑)

scarf

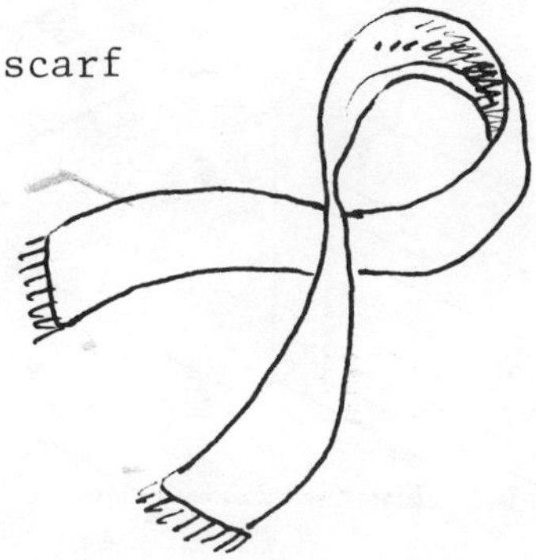

mok-do-ri (목도리)

boot(s)

chang-hwa (장화)

bathing suit

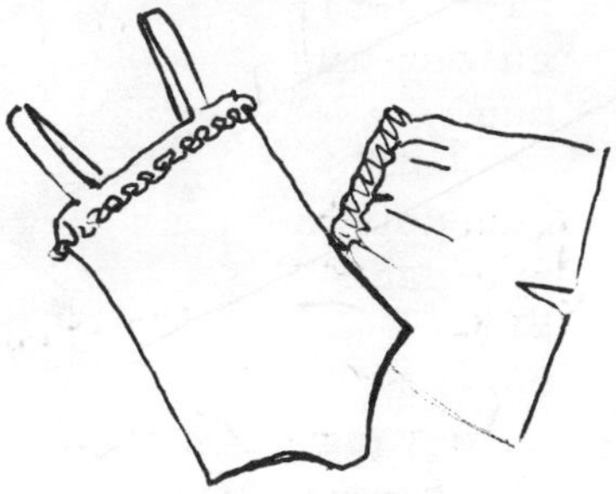

su-yŏng-bok (수영복)

mitten(s)

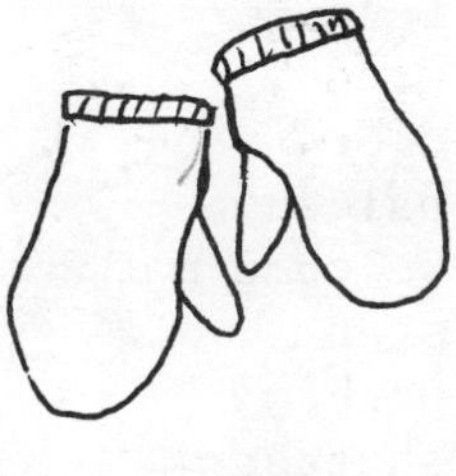

pŏng-ŏ-ri chang-gap
(벙어리장갑)

coat

oe-t'u (외투)

belt

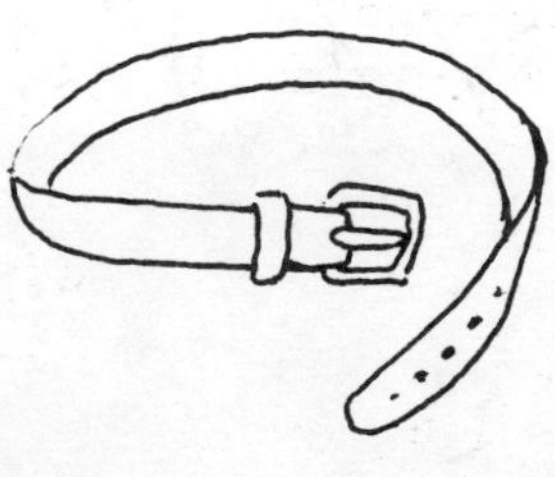

hyŏk-dae (혁대)

pants

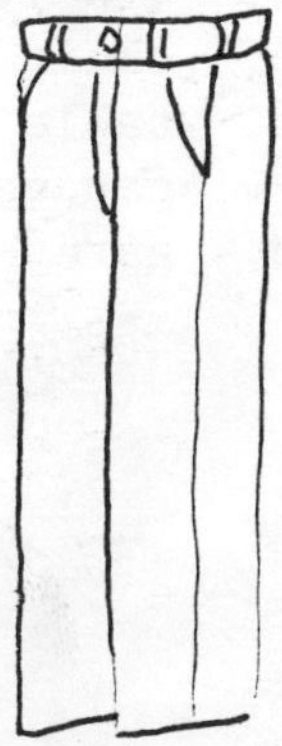

p'aen-ch'ŭ (팬츠)

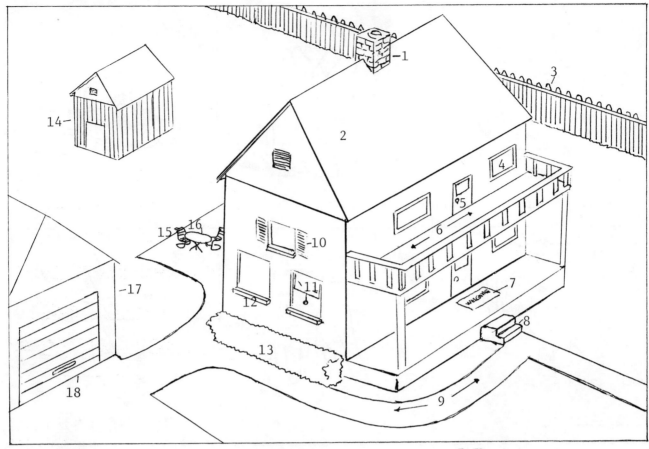

| | | | |
|---|---|---|---|
| 1. | chimney | kul-dduk | 굴뚝 |
| 2. | roof | chi-bung | 지붕 |
| 3. | fence | ul-t'a-ri | 울타리 |
| 4. | window | ch'ang-mun | 창문 |
| 5. | door | mun | 문 |
| 6. | balcony | no-dae | 노대 |
| 7. | welcome mat | mun-dot-ja-ri | 문돗자리 |
| 8. | step | kye-dan | 계단 |
| 9. | path | kil | 길 |
| 10. | shutter | tŏt-mun | 덧문 |
| 11. | shade | ch'a-yang | 차양 |
| 12. | window box | ch'ang-mun tong | 창문통 |
| 13. | bush | kwan-mok | 관목 |
| 14. | (tool) shed | (to-gu) hŏt-gan | 헛간 |
| 15. | chair | ŭi-ja | 의자 |
| 16. | table | t'ak-ja | 탁자 |
| 17. | garage | ch'a-go | 차고 |
| 18. | garage door | ch'a-go mun | 차고문 |

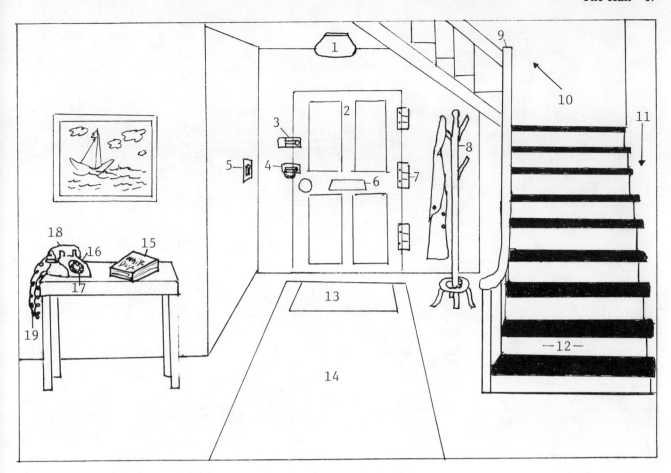

| | | | |
|---|---|---|---|
| 1. | (lamp) light | pul, jŏn-tŭng | 불,전등 |
| 2. | door | mun | 문 |
| 3. | bolt | na-sa | 나사 |
| 4. | lock and chain | cha-mul-soe | 자물쇠 |
| 5. | (light) switch | sŭ-wi-ch'i | 스위치 |
| 6. | mail slot | u-ch'e-mul ku-mŏng | 우체물 구멍 |
| 7. | hinge | tol-jjŏ-gwi | 돌쩌귀 |
| 8. | (coat) rack | (oe t'u) kŏ-ri | (외투)걸이 |
| 9. | banister | nan-gan-tong-ja | 난간동자 |
| 10. | upstairs | wi-ch'ŭng | 위층 |
| 11. | downstairs | a-rae-ch'ŭng | 아래층 |
| 12. | step | kye-dan | 계단 |
| 13. | doormat | mun-dae-ja-ri | 문대자리 |
| 14. | rug | yang-t'an-ja | 양탄자 |
| 15. | telephone directory | chŏn-hwa bu | 전화부 |
| 16. | telephone | chŏn-hwa | 전화 |
| 17. | dial | su-cha-p'an | 수자판 |
| 18. | receiver | su-hwa-gi | 수화기 |
| 19. | cord | chul | 줄 |

| | | | |
|---|---|---|---|
| 1. | ceiling | ch'ŏn-jang | 천장 |
| 2. | wall | pyŏk | 벽 |
| 3. | picture | kŭ-rim | 그림 |
| 4. | couch/sofa | kin-ŭi-ja | 긴의자 |
| 5. | lamp shade | tŭng-kat | 등갓 |
| 6. | lamp | tŭng | 등 |
| 7. | end table | kkŭt-tak-ja | 끝탁자 |
| 8. | chair | ŭi-ja | 의자 |
| 9. | coffee table | k'o-o-p'i t'ak-ja | 코오피탁자 |
| 10. | ashtray | chae-ddŏ-ri | 재떨이 |
| 11. | newspaper | sin-mun | 신문 |
| 12. | mirror | kŏ-ul | 거울 |
| 13. | mantel | pyŏk-nal-lo-sŏn-ban | 벽난로선반 |
| 14. | fireplace | pyŏk-nal-lo | 벽난로 |
| 15. | floor | ma-ru | 마루 |
| 16. | bookcase | ch'aek-chang | 책장 |
| 17. | book | ch'aek | 책 |
| 18. | shelf | sŏn-ban | 선반 |
| 19. | stereo | chŏn-chuk | 전축 |
| 20. | television/TV | t'e-ri-bi-jyŏn | 테리비젼 |
| 21. | drapery | p'o-jang | 포장 |
| 22. | armchair | al-lak-ŭi-ja | 안락의자 |
| 23. | money | ton | 돈 |
| 24. | letter | p'yŏn-ji | 편지 |

| 1.  | cupboard      | ch'an-jang                  | 찬장          |
| 2.  | can opener    | kkang-t'ong yŏ-nŭn-kigu     | 깡통 여는 기구  |
| 3.  | breadbox      | ppang-t'ong                 | 빵통          |
| 4.  | toaster       | t'o-sŭ-t'ŭ                  | 토스트        |
| 5.  | pan           | nam-bi                      | 남비          |
| 6.  | pot           | (so-gi-ki-p'ŭn) nam-bi      | (속이깊은)남비 |
| 7.  | stove         | nal-lo                      | 난로          |
| 8.  | kettle        | chu-jŏn-ja                  | 주전자        |
| 9.  | oven          | sot                         | 솥            |
| 10. | curtain       | k'ŏ-t'ŭn                    | 커어튼        |
| 11. | sink          | su-ch'ae                    | 수채          |
| 12. | dishcloth     | chŏp-si-su-gŏn              | 접시 수건     |
| 13. | dishwasher    | chop-si-ssit-nŭn ki-gu      | 접시 씻는 기구 |
| 14. | garbage can   | ssu-re-gi-t'ong             | 쓰레기 통     |
| 15. | refrigerator  | naeng-jang-go               | 냉장고        |
| 16. | chair         | ŭi-ja                       | 의자          |
| 17. | table         | sik-t'ak                    | 식탁          |
| 18. | fork          | p'o-k'ŭ                     | 포오크        |
| 19. | plate         | chŏp-si                     | 접시          |
| 20. | knife         | na-i-p'u, k'al              | 나이프, 칼     |
| 21. | spoon         | sut-ka-rak                  | 숟가락        |
| 22. | napkin        | naep-k'in                   | 냅킨          |
| 23. | saltshaker    | so-gŭm-pyŏng                | 소금병        |
| 24. | pepper shaker | hu-ch'u-pyŏng               | 후추병        |
| 25. | glass         | yu-ri-k'ŏp                  | 유리컵        |
| 26. | teacup        | ch'a-jan                    | 차잔          |
| 27. | sugar bowl    | sŏl-t'ang kŭ-rŭt            | 설탕그릇      |

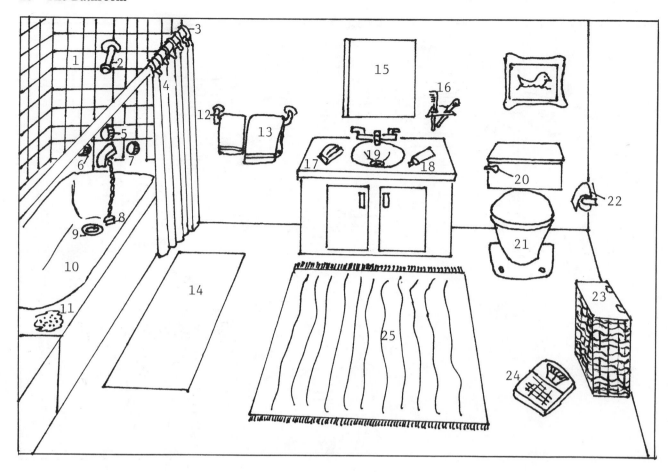

| | | | |
|---|---|---|---|
| 1. | title | t'a-il | 타일 |
| 2. | shower head | sya-uŏ mŏ-ri | 샤워머리 |
| 3. | curtain rod | hwi-jang tae | 휘장대 |
| 4. | shower curtain | sya-uŏ hwi-jang | 샤워휘장 |
| 5. | diverter | chŏn-hwan kkok-ch'i | 전환꼭지 |
| 6. | hot water faucet | tŏ-un-mul kkok-ch'i | 더운물꼭지 |
| 7. | cold water faucet | ch'an-mul kkok-ch'i | 찬물꼭지 |
| 8. | drain plug | pae-su ma-gae | 배수마개 |
| 9. | drain | pae-su | 배수 |
| 10. | bathtub | mok-yok-t'ong | 목욕통 |
| 11. | sponge | sŭ-p'ŏn-ji | 스펀지 |
| 12. | towel rack | su-gŏn gŏ-ri | 수건걸이 |
| 13. | towel | su-gŏn | 수건 |
| 14. | bath mat | mok-yok tot-ja-ri | 목욕돗자리 |
| 15. | medicine cabinet | yak-chang | 약장 |
| 16. | toothbrush | ch'it-sol | 칫솔 |
| 17. | soap | pi-nu | 비누 |
| 18. | toothpaste | ch'i-yak | 치약 |
| 19. | sink | su-ch'ae | 수채 |
| 20. | handle | son-ja-bi | 손잡이 |
| 21. | toilet | pyŏn-so | 변소 |
| 22. | toilet paper | hyu-ji | 휴지 |
| 23. | hamper | se-t'ak-mul tong | 세탁물통 |
| 24. | (bathroom) scale | (mok-tok-sil) chŏ-ul | (목욕실)저울 |
| 25. | rug | yang-t'an-ja | 얀탄자 |

| | | | |
|---|---|---|---|
| 1. | closet | pyŏk-jang | 벽장 |
| 2. | alarm clock | cha-myŏng-jong | 자명종 |
| 3. | night table | chŏ-nyŏk-t'ak-ja | 저녁탁자 |
| 4. | bed | ch'im-dae | 침대 |
| 5. | headboard | mŏ-ri-p'an | 머리판 |
| 6. | pillowcase | pe-gae-tŏp-gae | 베개덮개 |
| 7. | pillow | pe-gae | 베개 |
| 8. | mattress | mae-t'ŭ-ri-sŭ | 매트리스 |
| 9. | sheet | hot-i-bul | 홑이불 |
| 10. | blanket | tam-yo | 담요 |
| 11. | bedspread | ch'im-dae-bo | 침대보 |
| 12. | chest of drawers | ot-jang | 옷장 |
| 13. | mirror | kŏ-ul | 거울 |
| 14. | jewelry box | po-sŏk-sang-ja | 보석상자 |
| 15. | dressing table | hwa-jang-dae | 화장대 |
| 16. | comb | pit | 빗 |
| 17. | hair brush | mŏ-ri-sol | 머리솔 |
| 18. | stool | kŏl-sang | 걸상 |
| 19. | desk | ch'aek-sang | 책상 |
| 20. | chair | ŭi-ja | 의자 |
| 21. | doll | in-hyŏng | 인형 |
| 22. | ball | kong | 공 |
| 23. | skates | sŭ-k'ei-tŭ ku-du | 스케이트구두 |
| 24. | whistle | hwi-p'a-ram | 휘파람 |
| 25. | game | yu-hŭi, no-ri | 유희, 놀이 |
| 26. | rug | yang-t'an-ja | 양탄자 |

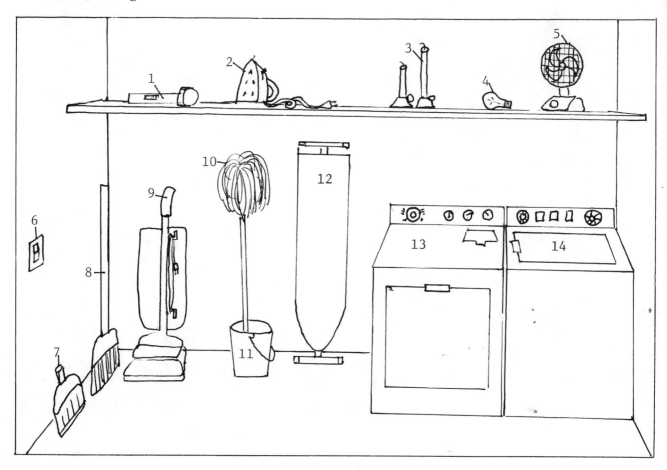

| | | |
|---|---|---|
| 1. flashlight | hoe-chung-chŭn-tŭng | 회중전등 |
| 2. iron | ta-ri-mi | 다리미 |
| 3. candle | ch'o | 초 |
| 4. (light) bulb | chŏn-gu | 전구 |
| 5. electric fan | sŏn-p'ung-gi | 선풍기 |
| 6. switch | sŭ-wi-ch'i | 스위치 |
| 7. dustpan | ssŭ-re-pat-ki | 쓰레받기 |
| 8. broom | pi | 비 |
| 9. vacuum cleaner | chŏn-gi so-je-gi | 전기소제기 |
| 10. mop | cha-ru kŏl-le | 자루걸레 |
| 11. bucket/pail | mul-t'ong | 물통 |
| 12. ironing board | ta-ri-mi-p'an | 다리미판 |
| 13. dryer | ot-mal-li-nŭn-ki-gu | 옷말리는기구 |
| 14. washing machine | se-t'ak-gi | 세탁기 |

| | | | |
|---|---|---|---|
| 1. | leaves | ip | 잎 |
| 2. | tree | na-mu | 나무 |
| 3. | fence | ul-t'a-ri | 울타리 |
| 4. | sidewalk | po-do | 보도 |
| 5. | gate | tae-mun | 대문 |
| 6. | vegetable garden | ch'ae-so bat | 채소밭 |
| 7. | flower | kkot | 꽃 |
| 8. | flower pot | hwa-bun | 화분 |
| 9. | door | mun | 문 |
| 10. | cat | ko-yang-i | 고양이 |
| 11. | sandbox | mo-rae-tong | 모래통 |
| 12. | dog | kae | 개 |
| 13. | clothesline | ppal-lae-jul | 빨래줄 |
| 14. | laundry | ppal-lae | 빨래 |
| 15. | swing | kŭ-ne | 그네 |
| 16. | grass | p'ul | 풀 |

A.   At the Dentist

| | | | |
|---|---|---|---|
| 1. | dental assistant | ch'i-kwa jo-su | 치과 조수 |
| 2. | lamp/light | chŏn-tŭng | 전등 |
| 3. | drill | ch'ak-kong-gi | 착공기 |
| 4. | dentist's chair | ch'i-kwa-ŭi-ja | 치과 의자 |
| 5. | dentist | ch'i-kwa-ŭi-sa | 치과 의사 |

B.   A Hospital Ward

| | | | |
|---|---|---|---|
| 6. | doctor | ŭi-sa | 의사 |
| 7. | stethoscope | ch'ŏng-jin-gi | 청진기 |
| 8. | nurse | kan-ho-wŏn | 간호원 |
| 9. | patient | hwan-ja | 환자 |
| 10. | bandage | pung-dae | 붕대 |
| 11. | bed | ch'im-dae | 침대 |

| | | | |
|---|---|---|---|
| 1. | (classroom) door | (kyo-sil) mun | 문 |
| 2. | clock | si-gye | 시계 |
| 3. | calendar | tal-ryŏk | 달력 |
| 4. | map | chi-do | 지도 |
| 5. | bulletin board | ke-si-p'an | 게시판 |
| 6. | teacher | sŏn-saeng-nim | 선생님 |
| 7. | blackboard | ch'il-p'an | 칠판 |
| 8. | eraser | chi-u-gae | 지우개 |
| 9. | student | hak-saeng | 학생 |
| 10. | chalk | paek-muk | 백묵 |
| 11. | notebook | kong-ch'aek | 공책 |
| 12. | book | ch'aek | 책 |
| 13. | chair | ŭi-ja | 의자 |
| 14. | classmate | tong-gŭp-saeng | 동급생 |
| 15. | ruler | cha | 자 |
| 16. | scissors | ka-wi | 가위 |
| 17. | crayons | k'ŭ-re-yong | 크레용 |
| 18. | glue | p'ul | 풀 |
| 19. | pencil | yŏn-p'il | 연필 |

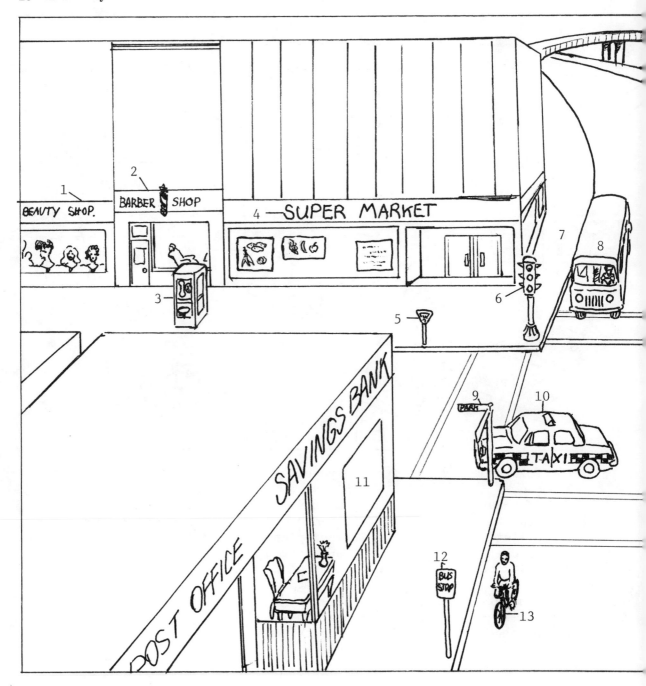

| | | | |
|---|---|---|---|
| 1. | beauty shop | mi-jang-wŏn | 미장원 |
| 2. | barbershop | i-bal-so | 이발소 |
| 3. | telephone booth | kong-jung chŏn-hwa | 공중전화 |
| 4. | supermarket | su-pŏ-ma-ket | 수퍼마켓 |
| 5. | parking meter | chu-ch'a kye-ryang-gi | 주차계량기 |
| 6. | traffic light | kyo-t'ong sin-ho-tŭng | 교통신호등 |
| 7. | sidewalk | po-do | 보도 |
| 8. | bus | pŏ-sŭ | 버스 |
| 9. | street sign | kŏ-ri p'yo-si | 거리표시 |
| 10. | taxi | t'aek-si | 택시 |
| 11. | bank | ŭn-haeng | 은행 |
| 12. | bus stop | pŏ-sŭ chŏng-ryu-so | 버스정류소 |
| 13. | bicycle | cha-jŏn-gŏ | 자전거 |

| | | | |
|---|---|---|---|
| 14. | bridge | ta-ri | 다리 |
| 15. | park | kong-wŏn | 공원 |
| 16. | street | kŏ-ri | 거리 |
| 17. | street lamp/light | ka-ro tŭng | 가로등 |
| 18. | hospital | pyŏng-wŏn | 병원 |
| 19. | parking ramp | chu-ch'a-jang | 주차장 |
| 20. | subway | chi-ha ch'ŏl | 지하철 |
| 21. | mailbox | u-ch'e-t'ong | 우체통 |
| 22. | motorcyle | o-t'o-ba-i | 오토바이 |
| 23. | department store | paek-hwa-jŏm | 백화점 |
| 24. | baby carriage | yu-mo-ch'a | 유모차 |
| 25. | trash can | ssŭ-re-gi tong | 쓰레기통 |
| 26. | drain/sewer | bae-su/su-ch'ae | 배스/수채 |
| 27. | car | cha-dong-ch'a | 자동차 |

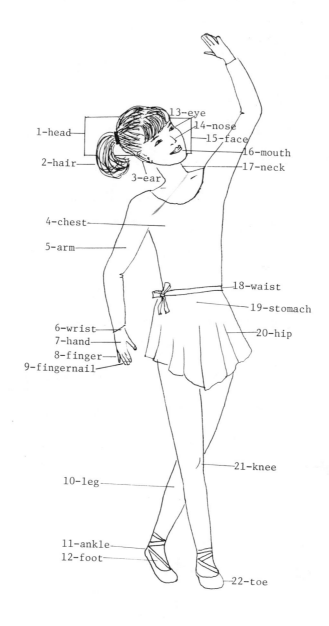

| 1. | head | mŏ-ri | 머리 | 12. | foot | pal | 발 |
| 2. | hair | mŏ-ri-t'ŏl | 머리털 | 13. | eye | nun | 눈 |
| 3. | ear | kwi | 귀 | 14. | nose | k'o | 코 |
| 4. | chest | ka-sŭm | 가슴 | 15. | face | ŏl-gul | 얼굴 |
| 5. | arm | p'al | 팔 | 16. | mouth | ip | 입 |
| 6. | wrist | son-mok | 손목 | 17. | neck | mok | 목 |
| 7. | hand | son | 손 | 18. | waist | hŏ-ri | 허리 |
| 8. | finger | son-ga-rak | 손가락 | 19. | stomach | pae | 배 |
| 9. | fingernail | son-t'op | 손톱 | 20. | hip | ŏng-dŏng-i | 엉덩이 |
| 10. | leg | ta-ri | 다리 | 21. | knee | mu-rŭp | 무릎 |
| 11. | ankle | pal-mok | 발목 | 22. | toe | pal-ga-rak | 발가락 |

| | | |
|---|---|---|
| address | chu-so | 주소 |
| adult | ŏ-rŭn | 어른 |
| animal | tong-mul | 동물 |
| another one | ta-rŭn-gŏt | 다른 것 |
| appointment | yak-sok | 약속 |
| baby | ae-gi | 애기 |
| back (of the body) | tŭng | 등 |
| back door | twit-mun | 뒷문 |
| basement | chi-ha-sil | 지하실 |
| beach | hae-byŏn-ka | 해변가 |
| beef | so-ko-gi | 소고기 |
| beginning | si-jak | 시작 |
| bell | chong | 종 |
| bird | sae | 새 |
| birthday | saeng-il | 생일 |
| bookstore | ch'aek-bang , sŏ-jŏm | 책방 , 서점 |
| building | kŭn-mul | 건물 |
| child | a-i | 아이 |
| church | kyo-hoe | 교회 |
| cigarette | tam-bae | 담배 |
| city | to-si | 도시 |
| clergyman | mok-sa | 목사 |
| country | nara, si-gol, kyo-oe | 나라, 시골, 교외 |
| cousin | sa-chon | 사촌 |
| crib | ae-gi-ch'im-dae | 애기침대 |
| daughter | ttal | 딸 |
| daytime | nat | 낮 |
| dictionary | sa-jŏn | 사전 |
| disease | pyŏng | 병 |
| earth | chi-gu | 지구 |
| east | tong-jjok | 동쪽 |
| education | kyo-yuk | 교육 |
| effort | no-ryŏk | 노력 |
| elder | son-wit sa-ram | 손윗 사람 |
| envelope | pong-t'u | 봉투 |
| error | chal-mot | 잘못 |
| essay | non-mun | 논문 |
| everybody | nu-gu-na | 누구나 |
| everyday | mae-il | 매일 |
| everything | mu-ŏ-si-dŭn-ji | 무엇이든지 |
| examination | si-hŏm | 시험 |
| exchange | kyo-hwan | 교환 |
| exercise | un-dong | 운동 |
| family | ka-jok | 가족 |
| faucet | su-do kkok-chi | 수도꼭지 |
| feeling | nŭ-kkim, ki-bun | 느낌, 기분 |
| female | yŏ-sŏng | 여성 |
| fire | pul | 불 |
| flag | ki | 기 |
| food | ŭm-sik | 음식 |
| friend | ch'in-gu | 친구 |
| front door | ap-mun | 앞문 |
| fruit | kwa-il | 과일 |

| fun | chae-mi | 재미 |
| furniture | ka-gu | 가구 |
| future | chang-rae | 장래 |
| | | |
| garden | ttŭl | 뜰 |
| garlic | ma-nŭl | 마늘 |
| gift | sŏn-mul | 선물 |
| gold | kŭm | 금 |
| good time | cho-ŭn si-gan | 좋은 시간 |
| grade | tŭng-gŭp | 등급 |
| grandchild | son-ja | 손자 |
| | | |
| habit | pŏ-rŭt | 버릇 |
| handkerchief | son-su-gŏn | 손수건 |
| help | to-um | 도움 |
| homework | suk-je | 숙제 |
| horse | mal | 말 |
| husband | nam-p'yŏn | 남편 |
| | | |
| I | nae-ga, na-nŭn | 내가, 나는 |
| ice | ŏ-rŭm | 어름 |
| idea | saeng-gak | 생각 |
| income | su-ip | 수입 |
| island | sŏm | 섬 |
| | | |
| job | il | 일 |
| joy | ki-bbŭm | 기쁨 |
| | | |
| key | yŏl-soe | 열쇠 |
| kindergarten | yu-ch'i-wŏn | 유치원 |
| | | |
| left | oen-p'yon | 왼편 |
| lesson | kyo-gwa, kyo-sŭp | 교과, 교습 |
| library | to-sŏ-gwan | 도서관 |
| life | saeng-myŏng | 생명 |
| | | |
| market | si-jang | 시장 |
| mealtime | sik-sa-si-gan | 식사시간 |
| medicine | yak | 약 |
| money | ton | 돈 |
| month | tal | 달 |
| | | |
| orphan | ko-a | 고아 |
| orphanage | ko-a-wŏn | 고아원 |
| | | |
| parent | pu-mo | 부모 |
| photograph | sa-jin | 사진 |
| price | kap | 값 |
| | | |
| school | hak-kyo | 학교 |
| she | kŭ-yŏ-ja | 그여자 |
| ship | pae | 배 |
| shop | chŏn-pang | 전방 |
| skin | ggŏp-jil | 껍질 |
| smell | naem-sae | 냄새 |
| smoke | yŏn-gi | 연기 |
| son | a-dŭl | 아들 |
| song | no-rae | 노래 |
| stamp | u-p'yo | 우표 |
| stocking(s) | kin-yang-mal | 긴 양말 |
| stone | tol | 돌 |

| | | |
|---|---|---|
| storm | p'ok-p'ung-u | 폭풍우 |
| story | i-ya-gi | 이야기 |
| string | kkŭn | 끈 |
| sunlight | haet-bit | 햇빛 |
| sunset | chŏ-nyŏk-nol | 저벽놀 |
| surgery | su-sul | 수술 |
| sweat | ttam | 땀 |
| tea | ch'a | 차 |
| teacher | sŏn-saeng | 선생 |
| tear(s) | nun-mul | 눈물 |
| test | si-hŏm | 시험 |
| theatre | kŭk-chang | 극장 |
| they | kŭ-dŭl | 그들 |
| thread | sil | 실 |
| time | si-gan | 시간 |
| today | o-nŭl | 오늘 |
| tomorrow | nae-il | 내일 |
| tonight | o-nŭl-pam | 오늘밤 |
| total | ch'ong-gye | 총계 |
| toy | chang-nam-kam | 장남간 |
| traffic | kyo-t'ong | 교통 |
| trash | ssŭ-re-gi | 쓰레기 |
| trip | yŏ-haeng | 여행 |
| umbrella | u-san | 우산 |
| university | tae-hak-kyo | 대학교 |
| vacation | hyu-ga | 휴가 |
| vaccination | ye-bang-chu-sa | 예방주사 |
| vegetable(s) | ch'ae-so | 채소 |
| way | kil | 길 |
| we | u-ri-ga, u-ri-nŭn | 우리가, 우리는 |
| wife | a-nae | 아내 |
| wind | pa-ram | 바람 |
| word | mal | 말 |
| world | se-gye | 세계 |
| year | hae | 해 |
| yesterday | ŏ-je | 어제 |
| you | tang-sin, nŏ | 당신, 너 |

## Verbs

| | | |
|---|---|---|
| arrive | to-ch'ak-ha-da | 도착하다 |
| asleep | cha-go-it-da | 자고 있다 |
| awake | kkae-da | 깨다 |
| bend | ku-bu-ri-da | 구부리다 |
| bite | mul-da | 물다 |
| bow | chŏl-ha-da | 절하다 |
| break | pu-su-da | 부수다 |
| brush (teeth) | takk-da | 닦다 |
| build | se-u-da | 세우다 |
| burn | t'ae-u-da | 태우다 |
| buy | sa-da | 사다 |
| can | hal-su-it-da | 할수 있다 |
| carry | un-ban-ha-da | 운반하다 |
| catch | chap-da | 잡다 |

| change | pa-kku-da | 바꾸다 |
| chew | ssip-da | 씹다 |
| climb | ki-ŏ-o-rŭ-da | 기어오르다 |
| close | tat-da | 닫다 |
| come | o-da | 오다 |
| comb | pit-da | 빗다 |
| cook | yo-ri-ha-da | 요리하다 |
| cough | ki-ch'im-ha-da | 기침하다 |
| count | se-da | 세다 |
| cry | ul-da | 울다 |
| cut | cha-rŭ-da | 자르다 |
| | | |
| dance | ch'um-ch'u-da | 춤추다 |
| dig | p'a-da | 파다 |
| discard | pŏ-ri-da | 버리다 |
| do | ha-da | 하다 |
| drink | ma-si-da | 마시다 |
| drive | un-jŏn-ha-da | 운전하다 |
| drop | ttŏ-rŏ-t'ŭ-ri-da | 떨어트리다 |
| | | |
| eat | mŏk-da | 먹다 |
| enjoy | chŭl-gi-da | 즐기다 |
| erase | chi-u-da | 지우다 |
| | | |
| fall | ttŏ-rŏ-ji-da | 떨어지다 |
| feel | nŭ-ggi-da | 느끼다 |
| fight | ssa-u-da | 싸우다 |
| fix | ko-chi-da | 고치다 |
| fly | nal-da | 날다 |
| fold | jŏp-da | 접다 |
| forget | i-jŏ-pŏ-ri-da | 잊어버리다 |
| | | |
| get up | i-rŏ-na-da | 일어나다 |
| give | ju-da | 주다 |
| go | ka-da | 가다 |
| | | |
| hang | kŏl-da | 걸다 |
| have | ka-ji-da | 가지다 |
| hit | ch'i-da | 치다 |
| hold | put-chap-da | 붙잡다 |
| hope | pa-ra-da | 바라다 |
| hug | kkyŏ-an-da | 껴안다 |
| hurt | a-p'ŭ-da | 아프다 |
| | | |
| jump | ttwi-da | 뛰다 |
| | | |
| kick | ch'a-da | 차다 |
| kiss | ip-mat-ch'u-da | 입맞추다 |
| | | |
| laugh | ut-da | 웃다 |
| learn | pae-u-da | 배우다 |
| leave | ttŏ-na-da | 떠나다 |
| listen | tŭt-da | 듣다 |
| lie down | nup-da | 눕다 |
| lose | il-t'a | 잃다 |
| love | sa-rang-ha-da | 사랑하다 |
| | | |
| make | man-dŭl-da | 만들다 |
| move | um-jig-i-da | 움직이다 |
| | | |
| need | p'i-ryo-ha-da | 필요하다 |

| | | |
|---|---|---|
| open | yŏl-da | 열다 |
| paint | kŭ-ri-da | 그리다 |
| peel | pŏt-gi-da | 벗기다 |
| play | nol-da | 놀다 |
| point | ka-ri-k'i-da | 가리키다 |
| pray | ki-do-ha-da | 기도하다 |
| pull | kkŭl-da | 끌다 |
| push | mil-da | 밀다 |
| put | no-t'a | 놓다 |
| read | ilk-da | 읽다 |
| rest | hyu-sik-ha-da | 휴식하다 |
| ride | t'a-da | 타다 |
| rise | o-rŏ-da | 오르다 |
| run | ttwi-ŏ-ka-da | 뛰어가다 |
| say | mal-ha-da | 말하다 |
| scratch | kŭlk-da | 긁다 |
| sell | p'al-da | 팔다 |
| sew | kip-da | 깁다 |
| show | po-i-da | 보이다 |
| shut | tat-da | 닫다 |
| sing | no-rae-ha-da | 노래하다 |
| sit | an-da | 앉다 |
| sleep | cha-da | 자다 |
| smile | mi-so-ha-da | 미소하다 |
| sneeze | chae-ch'ae-gi-ha-da | 재채기하다 |
| speak | mal-ha-da | 말하다 |
| spill | ŏp-chi-ru-da | 엎지르다 |
| stand | sŏ-da | 서다 |
| start | si-jak-ha-da | 시작하다 |
| stop | chung-ji-ha-da | 중지하다 |
| study | kong-bu-ha-da | 공부하다 |
| sweep | ssŭl-da | 쓸다 |
| swim | he-ŏm-ch'i-da | 헤엄치다 |
| take | chap-da | 잡다 |
| taste | mat-bo-da | 맛보다 |
| teach | ka-rŭ-ch'i-da | 가르치다 |
| tell | mal-ha-da | 말하다 |
| think | saeng-gak-ha-da | 생각하다 |
| throw | nae-dŏn-ji-da | 내던지다 |
| tie | mae-da | 매다 |
| touch | man-ji-da | 만지다 |
| turn | tol-ri-da | 돌리다 |
| understand | i-hae-ha-da | 이해하다 |
| use | ssŭ-da | 쓰다 |
| wait | ki-da-ri-da | 기다리다 |
| walk | kŏt-da | 걷다 |
| want | wŏn-ha-da | 원하다 |
| wash | ssit-da | 씻다 |
| waste | nang-bi-ha-da | 낭비하다 |
| wear | ip-da | 입다 |
| work | il-ha-da | 일하다 |
| worry | kŏk-chŏng-ha-da | 걱정하다 |
| write | ssŭ-da | 쓰다 |

| | | |
|---|---|---|
| angry | no-han | 노한 |
| anxious | kŏk-jŏng-ha-nun | 걱정하는 |
| anyone | nu-gu-na | 누구나 |
| back | twi-ŭi | 뒤의 |
| bad | na-bbŭn | 나쁜 |
| big/large | k'ŭn | 큰 |
| bright | pal-gŭn | 밝은 |
| careful | chu-ŭi-gi-p'ŭn | 주의깊은 |
| cheap | ssan | 싼 |
| clean | kkae-ggŭt-han | 깨끗한 |
| cold | ch'an | 찬 |
| comfortable | p'yŏn-an-han | 편안한 |
| dark | ŏ-du-un | 어두운 |
| dead | chu-gŭn | 죽은 |
| deep | ki-p'ŭn | 깊은 |
| dirty | tŏ-rŏ-un | 더러운 |
| dry | ma-rŭn | 마른 |
| dull | tun-han | 둔한 |
| early | i-rŭn | 이른 |
| easy | swi-un | 쉬운 |
| empty | pin | 빈 |
| expensive | pi-ssan | 비싼 |
| fat | sal-jjin | 살찐 |
| fast | ppa-rŭn | 빠른 |
| first | ch'ŏt-jjae-ŭi | 첫째의 |
| fresh | sin-sŏn-han | 신선한 |
| front | a-p'ŭi | 앞의 |
| full | ka-dŭk-ch'an | 가득찬 |
| good | cho-hŭn | 좋은 |
| great | kŏ-dae-han | 거대한 |
| happy | ki-bbŭn | 기쁜 |
| hard | ŏ-ryŏ-un | 어려운 |
| heavy | mu-gŏ-un | 무거운 |
| high | no-p'ŭn | 높은 |
| hot | ttŭ-gŏ-un | 뜨거운 |
| hungry | pae-go-p'ŭn | 배고픈 |
| important | chung-yo-han | 중요한 |
| interesting | chae-mi-it-nŭn | 재미있는 |
| kind | ch'in-jŏl-han | 친절한 |
| large | k'ŭn | 큰 |
| last | ch'oe-hu-ŭi | 최후의 |
| left | oen-jjok-ŭi | 왼쪽의 |
| light | ka-byŏ-un | 가벼운 |
| little/small | cha-gŭn | 작은 |
| long | kin | 긴 |
| loose | hŏl-gŏ-un | 헐거운 |
| loud | so-ri-no-p'ŭn | 소리높은 |
| low | na-jŭn | 낮은 |

| | | |
|---|---|---|
| many | man-ŭn | 많은 |
| narrow | cho-bŭn | 좁은 |
| near | ka-gga-un | 가까운 |
| neat | tan-jŏng-han | 단정한 |
| new | sae-ro-un | 새로운 |
| old/used | hŏn | 헌 |
| once | han-bŏn | 한번 |
| possible | ka-nŭng-han | 가능한 |
| right | o-rŭn-jjok-ŭi | 오른쪽의 |
| rough | kŏ-ch'in | 거친 |
| sad | sŭl-p'ŭn | 슬픈 |
| safe | an-jŏn-han | 안전한 |
| same | ka-t'ŭn | 같은 |
| shallow | ya-t'ŭn | 얕은 |
| sharp | nal-k'a-ro-un | 날카로운 |
| short | jjal-bŭn | 짧은 |
| slow | nŭ-rin | 느린 |
| small/little | cha-gŭn | 작은 |
| smooth | mae-ggŭ-rŏ-un | 매끄러운 |
| soft | pu-dŭ-rŏ-un | 부드러운 |
| solid | tan-dan-han | 단단한 |
| some | ŏ-ddŏn | 어떤 |
| sore | a-p'ŭn | 아픈 |
| straight | ttok-ba-rŭn | 똑바른 |
| strong | kang-han | 강한 |
| tall | k'i-ga-k'ŭn | 키가큰 |
| thick | tu-ggŏ-un | 두꺼운 |
| thin | yŏ-win | 여윈 |
| tight | p'aeng-p'aeng-han | 팽팽한 |
| tough | ŏk-sen | 억센 |
| true | jin-sil-han | 진실한 |
| twice | tu-bŏn | 두번 |
| useful | yu-yong-han | 유용한 |
| very | tae-dan-hi | 대단히 |
| weak | yak-han | 약한 |
| wet | chŏ-jŭn | 젖은 |
| when | ŏn-je | 언제 |
| where | ŏ-di-e | 어디에 |
| wide | nŏl-bŭn | 넓은 |
| young | chŏl-mŭn | 젊은 |

## Greetings and Civilties

| Good morning! | An-yŏng-hi-cha-sŭm-ni-ka? | 안녕히 잤읍니까? |
| Good afternoon! | An-nyŏng-ha-sim-ni-ka? | 안녕하십니까? |
| Good night! | An-yŏng-hi-cha-se-yo. | 안녕히자세요? |

| Hello! | Yŏ-bo-se-yo! | 여보세요! |
| How are you! | An-nyŏng-ha-se-yo? | 안녕하세요? |
| I'm fine. | Cho-sŭm-ni-da. | 좋습니다. |

| My name is Anne. | Na-ŭi-i-rŭm-ŭn-Anne-im-ni-da. | 나의이름은앤입니다. |
| I'm glad to meet you. | Man-na-sŏ-pan-gap-sŭm-ni-da. | 만나서 반갑습니다. |
| I'm happy you came. | Nŏ-ga-wa-sŏ-ki-bbŏ-da. | 너가 와서 기쁘다. |

| Have a good day. | Cho-ŭn-na-rŭl ka-ji-se-yo. | 좋은날을 가지세요. |
| Have a good time. | Chae-mi-it-ge-chi-ne-se-yo. | 재미있게지내세요. |
| Come back soon. | Kot-tora-o-se-yo. | 곧돌아오세요. |
| I'll come back soon. | Kot-tora-o-get-sŏ-yo. | 곧돌아오겠어요. |
| I'm home. | Chip-e to-ra-wat-sŭm-ni-da. | 집에돌아왔읍니다. |
| Did you have good time? | Chae-mi it-sŏt-sŭm-ni-ca? | 재미있었읍니까? |

| Thank you. | Kam-sa-ham-ni-da | 감사합니다. |
| You are welcome. | Chŏn-man-e-yo. | 천만에요. |
| I am sorry. | Mi-an-ham-ni-da. | 미안합니다. |
| Forgive me. | Yong-sŏ-ha-se-yo. | 용서하세요. |
| Excuse me/ pardon me. | Sil-rye-ham-ni-da. | 실례합니다. |

| Goodbye. | An-nyŏng-hi-kye-sip-si-yo. | 안녕히계십시요. |

## Mealtime

| Let us eat. | Mŏk-ja. | 먹자. |
| Let us have breakfast. | A-ch'im-pap-ŭl mŏk-ja. | 아침밥을먹자. |
| Let us have lunch. | Chŏm-sim-ŭl mŏk-ja. | 점심을먹자. |
| Let us have dinner. | Chŏ-nyŏk-pap-ŭl mŏk-ja. | 저녁밥을먹자. |

| It's time for lunch. | Chŏm-sim-ttae-da. | 점심때다. |
| Are you hungry? | Pae-ko-p'ŭ-ni? | 배고프니? |
| I'm hungry. | Pae-ko-p'ŭ-da. | 배고프다. |
| Are you full? | Pae-ga-ch'an-ni? | 배가찬니? |
| Do you like this? | I-gŏ-sŭl-cho-a-ha-ni? | 이것을좋아하니? |
| Try some of this. | I-gŏ-sŭl-mŏ-gŭ-se-yo. | 이것을먹으세요. |
| Do you want some more? | Tŏ-mŏk-go-sip-ni? | 더먹고싶니? |
| It's delicious. | Ma-si-it-da. | 맛이있다. |

## Personal Care

| | | |
|---|---|---|
| Wash your hands. | Son-ŭl ssi-sŏ-yo. | 손을 씻어요. |
| Wash your face. | Ŏl-gul-ŭl ssi-sŏ-yo. | 얼굴을 씻어요. |
| Wash your hair. | Mŏ-ri-rŭl ssi-sŏ-yo. | 머리를 씻어요. |
| Brush your teeth. | I-rŭl ta-kkŭ-se-yo. | 이를 닦으세요. |
| Comb your hair. | Mŏ-ri-rŭl pit-sŏ-yo. | 머리를 빗어요. |
| Take a bath. | Mok-yok-ŭl hea. | 목욕을해. |
| Do you want to go to the bathroom? | Pyŏn-so-e ka-go-si-pŏ? | 변소에가고싶어? |
| You need a haircut? | Mŏri-rŭl ka-kka-ya-get-da. | 머리를 깎아야겠다. |
| Let's go to a barbershop. | I-bal-so-e ka-ja. | 이발소에 가자. |
| Let's go to a beauty shop. | Mi-jang-wŏn-e ka-ja. | 미장원에 가자. |

## Heath Care

| | | |
|---|---|---|
| I feel sick. | Ki-bun-i cho-ch'i-an-sŭm-ni-da. | 기분이 좋지않습니다. |
| I have a headache. | Mŏ-ri-ga a-p'ŭm-ni-da. | 머리가 아픕니다. |
| I have an upset stomach. | Pae-ga a-p'ŭm-ni-da. | 배가아픔니다. |
| I feel nauseated. | T'o-hal-ki-bun-im-ni-da. | 토할 기분입니다. |
| I have a pain here. | Yŏ-gi-ga a-p'ŭm-ni-da. | 여기가아픔니다. |
| I have a toothache. | I-ga a-p'ŭm-ni-da. | 이가아픔니다. |
| I have an earache. | Kwi-ga a-p'ŭm-ni-da. | 귀가 아픔니다. |
| I have a sore throat. | Mo-gi a-p'ŭm-ni-da. | 목이아픔이다. |
| My arms hurt. | P'al-i a-p'ŭm-ni-da. | 팔이아픔니다. |
| Do you have a headache? | Mo-ri-ga a-p'ŭ-ni? | 머리가아프니? |
| Is your stomach upset? | Pae-ga a-p'ŭ-ni? | 배가아프니? |
| Do you have a cold? | Kam-gi-ga tŭ-rŏt-ni? | 감기가들었니? |

## In the School

| | | |
|---|---|---|
| This is our school. | I-gŏt-si u-ri-hak-kyo-i-da. | 이것이우리학교이다. |
| This is our classroom. | I-gŏt-si u-ri-kyo-sil-i-da. | 이것이우리교실이다. |
| (Please) sit down. | An-jŭ-se-yo. | 앉으세요. |
| (Please) stand up. | I-rŏ-na-se-yo. | 일어나세요. |
| (Please) open the book. | Ch'aek-ŭl yŏ-se-yo. | 책을 여세요. |
| (Please) read. | Ir-gŭ-se-yo. | 읽으세요. |
| (Please) write. | Ssŭ-se-yo. | 쓰세요. |
| (Please) repeat. | Toe-p'u-ri-ha-se-yo. | 되풀이하세요. |
| (Please) answer. | Tae-dap-ha-se-yo. | 대답하세요. |
| (Please) wait. | Ki-da-ri-se-yo. | 기다리세요. |
| You can go home. | Chip-e Ka-se-yo. | 집에 가세요. |
| What is this? | I-kŏ-si-mu-ŏ-si-ni? | 이것이무엇이니? |
| What is your name? | Nŏ-ui-i-rŭm-i mu-ŏ-si-ni? | 너의이름이무엇이니? |
| My name is Anne. | Na-ŭi-i-rŭm-un Anne-i-da. | 나의이름은 앤이다. |
| Where do you live? | Ŏ-di-e-sa-ni? | 어디에사니? |
| What is your address? | Nŏ-ŭi-chu-so-nŭn mu-ŏ-si-ni? | 너의주소는 무엇이니? |
| How old are you? | Myŏt-sal-i-ni? | 몇살이니? |
| (I'm) six years old. | Yo-sŏt-sal-i-da. | 여섯살이다. |
| Where is the bathroom? | Pyŏn-so-ga ŏ-di-it-ni? | 변소가어디있니? |

## Affective Communication

| | | |
|---|---|---|
| I love you. | Nŏ-rŭl sa-rang-hae. | 너를 사랑해. |
| I like you. | No-rŭl cho-a-hae. | 너를 좋아해. |
| I am glad. | Ki-bbŭ-da. | 기쁘다. |
| Do you like this? | I-gŏ-sŭl cho-a-ha-ni?? | 이것을 좋아하니? |
| Are you upset? | Haw-ga-nat-ni? | 화가 났니? |
| I am upset. | Hwa-ga-na. | 화가 나. |
| Are you tired? | P'i-gon-ha-ni? | 피곤하니? |
| I am tired. | P'i-gon-hae. | 피곤해. |
| Are you sad? | Sŭl-p'ŭ-ni? | 슬프니? |
| I am sad. | Sŭl-p'ŭ-da. | 슬프다. |
| Are you sleepy? | Chol-ri-ni? | 졸리니? |
| I am sleepy. | Chol-ri-da. | 졸리다. |

## Directive Communication

| | | |
|---|---|---|
| It's time to get up. | I-rŏ-nal si-gan-i-da. | 일어날 시간이다. |
| It's time to go to bed. | Chal si-gan-i-da. | 잘 시간이다. |
| Please come here. | I-ri-ro o-se-yo. | 이리로 오세요. |
| Give it to me. | Chu-se-yo. | 주세요. |
| Stop it. | Kŭ-man-hae. | 그만해. |
| Stand here. | Yŏ-gi sŏ-it-so. | 여기서 있어. |
| Wait here. | Yŏ-gi-e ki-ta-ryŏ. | 여기에 기다려. |
| Sit here. | Yŏ-gi-e an-jŭ-se-yo. | 여기에 앉으세요. |
| Be quiet. | Cho-yong-hi-hae. | 조용히 해. |
| Come with me. | Na-wa-ka-ch'i-wa. | 나와 같이 와. |
| Bring that here. | Kŭ-gŏ-sŭl ka-ji-go-wa. | 그것을 가지고 와. |
| Throw it away. | Kŏ-gŏ-sŭl pŏ-ri-ra. | 그것을 버리라. |
| Where are you going? | Ŏ-di-e ka-ni? | 어디에 가니? |
| What is this? | I-gŏ-si mu-ŏ-si-ni? | 이것이 무엇이니? |
| Good! | Cho-ta. | 좋다. |
| It's hot! | Ttŭ-gŏp-da. | 뜨겁다. |
| It's dangerous. | Wi-hŏm-hea. | 위험해. |
| Let's go home. | Chip-e ka-ja | 집에 가자. |
| Let's go to school. | Hak-kyo-e ka-ja. | 학교에 가자. |

## Time of Day

| | | |
|---|---|---|
| day | nal | 날 |
| morning | a-ch'im | 아침 |
| noon | chŏng-o | 정오 |
| afternoon | o-hu | 오후 |
| evening | chŏ-nyŏk | 저떡 |
| night | pam | 밤 |

## Weekdays

| | | |
|---|---|---|
| Monday | wŏ-ryo-il | 월요일 |
| Tuesday | hwa-yo-il | 화요일 |
| Wednesday | su-yo-il | 수요일 |
| Thursday | mo-gyo-il | 목요일 |
| Friday | kŭm-yo-il | 금요일 |
| Saturday | t'o-yo-il | 토요일 |
| Sunday | i-ryo-il | 일요일 |

## Months

| | | |
|---|---|---|
| January | chŏng-wŏl, i-rwŏl | 정월, 일월 |
| Febryary | i-wŏl | 이월 |
| March | sam-wŏl | 삼월 |
| April | sa-wŏl | 사월 |
| May | o-wŏl | 오월 |
| June | yu-wŏl | 유월 |
| July | ch'i-rwŏl | 칠월 |
| August | p'a-rwŏl | 팔월 |
| September | ku-wŏl | 구월 |
| October | si-wŏl | 시월 |
| November | sip-i-rwŏl | 십일월 |
| December | sip-i-wŏl | 십이월 |

## Seasons

| | | |
|---|---|---|
| spring | pom | 봄 |
| summer | yŏ-rŭm | 여름 |
| autumn | ka-ŭl | 가을 |
| winter | kyŏ-ŭl | 겨울 |

## Weather

| sunny day | haet-pyŏt-jjoe-nŭn-nal | 햇볕쬐는날 |
| cloudy day | hŭ-rin-nal | 흐린날 |
| rainy day | pi-o-nŭn-nal | 비오는날 |
| warm day | tta-ddŭt-han-nal | 따뜻한날 |
| hot day | tŏ-un-nal | 더운날 |
| cold day | ch'u-un-nal | 추운날 |
| cool day | sŏ-nŭl-han-nal | 서늘한날 |

| sky | ha-nŭl | 하늘 |
| sun | hae | 해 |
| rain | pi | 비 |
| cloud | ku-rŭm | 구름 |

| moon | tal | 달 |
| bright moon | pal-gŭn-tal | 밝은달 |
| half moon | pan-tal | 반달 |
| stars | pyŭl | 별 |

## Colors

| white | hŭin | 흰 |
| black | kŏm-ŭn | 검은 |
| pink | pun-hong | 분홍 |
| red | pul-gŭn | 붉은 |
| orange | o-ren-ji | 오렌지 |
| yellow | no-ran | 노란 |
| brown | kal-saek | 갈색 |
| green | ch'o-rok-saek | 초록색 |
| blue | p'u-rŭn | 푸른 |
| purple | cha-ju-bit | 자주빛 |

## Academic Subjects

| art | ye-sul | 예술 |
| arithmatic | san-su | 산수 |
| English | yŏng-o | 영어 |
| history | yŏk-sa | 역사 |
| mathematics | su-hak | 수학 |
| music | ŭm-ak | 음악 |
| physical education | ch'e-yuk | 체육 |
| reading | tok-sŏ | 독서 |
| science | kwa-hak | 과학 |
| social studies | sa-hoe-kwa-mok | 사회과목 |

## Korean Numerals

| | | | | |
|---|---|---|---|---|
| 1 | one | ha-na, han | 하나, 한 | |
| 2 | two | tul, tu | 둘, 두 | |
| 3 | three | set, se | 셋, 세 | |
| 4 | four | net, ne | 넷, 네 | |
| 5 | five | ta-sŏt | 다섯 | |
| 6 | six | yŏ-sŏt | 여섯 | |
| 7 | seven | il-gop | 일곱 | |
| 8 | eight | yŏ-dŏl | 여덟 | |
| 9 | nine | a-hop | 아홉 | |
| 10 | ten | yŏl | 열 | |
| 11 | eleven | yŏl-ha-na, yŏl-han | 열하나, 열한 | |
| 12 | twelve | yŏl-tul, yŏl-tu | 열둘, 열두 | |
| 13 | thirteen | yŏl-set, yŏl-se | 열셋, 열세 | |
| 14 | fourteen | yŏl-net, yŏl-ne | 열넷, 열네 | |
| 15 | fifteen | yŏl-ta-sŏt | 열다섯 | |
| 16 | sixteen | yŏl-yŏ-sŏt | 열여섯 | |
| 17 | seventeen | yŏl-il-gop | 열일곱 | |
| 18 | eighteen | yŏl-yŏ-dŏl | 열여덟 | |
| 19 | nineteen | yŏl-a-hop | 열아홉 | |
| 20 | twenty | sŭ-mul | 스물 | |
| 21 | twenty-one | sŭ-mul-hana, sŭ-mul-han | 스물하나, 스물한 | |
| 22 | twenty-two | sŭ-mul-tul, sŭ-mul-tu | 스물둘, 스물두 | |
| 23 | twenty-three | sŭ-mul-set, sŭ-mul-se | 스물셋, 스물세 | |
| 24 | twenty-four | sŭ-mul-net, sŭ-mul-ne | 스물넷, 스물네 | |
| 25 | twenty-five | sŭ-mul-ta-sŏt | 스물다섯 | |
| 26 | twenty-six | sŭ-mul-yŏ-sŏt | 스물여섯 | |

## Chinese Numerals

| | | | | | |
|---|---|---|---|---|---|
| 1 | one | il | 일 | | |
| 2 | two | i | 이 | | |
| 3 | three | sam | 삼 | | |
| 4 | four | sa | 사 | | |
| 5 | five | o | 오 | | |
| 6 | six | yuk | 육 | | |
| 7 | seven | ch'il | 칠 | | |
| 8 | eight | pa'l | 팔 | | |
| 9 | nine | ku | 구 | | |
| 10 | ten | sip | 십 | | |
| 11 | eleven | sip-il | 십일 | | |
| 12 | twelve | sip-i | 십이 | | |
| 13 | thirteen | sip-sam | 십삼 | | |
| 14 | fourteen | sip-sa | 십사 | | |
| 15 | fifteen | sip-o | 십오 | | |
| 16 | sixteen | sip-yuk | 십육 | | |
| 17 | seventeen | sip-ch'il | 십칠 | | |
| 18 | eighteen | sip-p'al | 십팔 | | |
| 19 | nineteen | sip-ku | 십구 | | |
| 20 | twenty | i-sip | 이십 | | |
| 21 | twenty-one | i-sip-il | 이십일 | | |
| 22 | twenty-two | i-sip-i | 이십이 | | |
| 23 | twenty-three | i-sip-sam | 이십삼 | | |
| 24 | twenty-four | i-sip-sa | 이십사 | | |
| 25 | twenty-five | i-sip-o | 이십오 | | |
| 26 | twenty-six | i-sip-yuk | 이십육 | | |

| Number | English | Korean | 한글 | Chinese | 한글 |
|---|---|---|---|---|---|
| 30 | thirty | sŏ-rŭn | 서른 | sam-sip | 삼십 |
| 40 | forty | ma-hŭn | 마흔 | sa-sip | 사십 |
| 50 | fifty | swin | 쉰 | o-sip | 오십 |
| 60 | sixty | ye-sŭn | 예순 | yuk-sip | 육십 |
| 70 | seventy | il-hŭn | 일흔 | ch'il-sip | 칠십 |
| 80 | eighty | yo-dŭn | 여든 | pa'l-sip | 팔십 |
| 90 | ninety | a-hŭn | 아흔 | ku-sip | 구십 |
| 100 | one-hundred | paek | 백 | paek | 백 |
| 200 | two-hundred | i-baek | 이백 | i-baek | 이백 |
| 300 | three-hundred | sam-baek | 삼백 | sam-baek | 삼백 |

Two sets of numerals, as listed above, are used in Korea; one is the native Korean numerals, and the other is borrowed from the Chinese. While the Chinese numerals are used in counting numbers, money, or minutes, the Korean numerals are used mostly in counting things, people, or hours, etc. Some of the Korean numerals change to simpler forms, when modifying things. For example, while 1 is ha-na, 1 o'clock is han si or 1 book is han ch'aek. Also, while the two sets of numerals are used up to 99, for 100 and above only the Chinese set is used.